"Deep and cutting at times, Vanderlaan takes us beyond the pain to where healing can be found. *Unspoken Confessions* is stunning in its clarity and depth."
– BETH-ANNE WHITE

"This book leaves me speechless at how real it is, speaking more truth every time I read it. This is not about men only; this is equally about women. It's a journey from sin to restoration. A unique standpoint and a must read!"
– ADELINA ALEXE

"Dark and refreshing. I don't read poetry as a rule, but in this case I'm glad I made an exception."
– MATTHEW J. LUCIO

"Thoughtful and artistic, but also packs a punch! This isn't the stuff you read on greeting cards."
– JESSICA M. SHIMER

"Deathly honest!"
– JASON MILLER

"Each poem is genuine and open, leaving no doubt in your mind that what you've just read is from the heart. This book is a calling to a higher standard and a better life – for both men and women."
– KRISTIN THOMAS

"Candid and honest about what men struggle with, the temptations they have, and the desire to overcome."
– AMBER HILL

THE DARKLIGHT SERIES

~ BOOK I ~

UNSPOKEN CONFESSIONS

T. JASON VANDERLAAN

BALM AND BLADE
PUBLISHING

ISBN: 978-0-9841386-1-6

Published by Balm and Blade Publishing
1475 Hollow Road
Birchrunville, PA 19421
www.balmandblade.com

Cover design by T. Jason Vanderlaan
www.jasonvanderlaan.com

For you – wherever you may be.

Contents

IV. To Turn Blind Eyes Towards the Light

V. Water For Our Hands, Blood For Our Souls

VI. The Way Back Starts Not With a Step, But With a Stand

P.S.

Acknowledgments

Introduction

This is not the first book I wanted to write.

I wanted to write a book that would endear me to you, something that would inspire you with its brilliance and make you want to read more of my writings.

Instead, you have this: a poetic exposition of some of my darkest secrets.

This book began in a university cafeteria in Tennessee. I had just started my senior year of college and had gone to get lunch. As I stood in line, I heard a couple guys behind me comparing their favorite actresses, describing the best assets of each (and it had nothing to do with their ability to act). I was shocked, not so much that they thought such things, but that they were speaking about them so openly in a public place.

You see, most guys spend inordinate amounts of time in college trying to impress girls. The basic premise behind this endeavor is to emphasize your best qualities and downplay your faults, even to the point of making them disappear. Thus, girls only get a one-sided picture of most guys.

Listening to the two guys behind me, I realized that many women do not know the darker side of men, or if they are aware of it they try to ignore it. What would happen if the secret thoughts and lives of men were really known? What if they really knew about all the pornography, or the thoughts we think, or the way we have treated other women?

And I'm not just talking about "those guys" who you'd expect this kind of stuff from. I'm talking about your best friends, your brothers, your boyfriends... the guys you'd never suspect. They harbor dark secrets as well. We all do.

I got my food, took a seat in the back corner of the dining area, and began to write what would eventually become this book. I wrote confessions of my own, confessions of other men I knew, confessions on behalf of all men. It was a thoroughly draining and discouraging work.

Let me be clear though: this book is not an attempt to discredit and slander all men. No, this is an attempt at honesty. This is an attempt to challenge men to face up to who they have become. This is an attempt to encourage women to raise their standards and settle for nothing less than a man of God.

And this is ultimately a book of hope. Of darkness, yes. But more importantly, of light in that darkness.

It is my prayer that when you have finished reading this book, your thoughts will not dwell on the failures of men, but on the great potential within us. If you are a woman, don't give up on us yet. If you are a man, don't give up on yourself, or on the God who can change your heart from stone to living, beating flesh.

You hold in your hands the unspoken confessions of a man, on behalf of men, for the benefit of men and those who love us or have loved us or will one day love us.

Tread softly upon this broken ground.

~ Jason

I.

What Our Eyes Have Seen

Beneath the Armor

Many women throughout history
Have been swept off their feet
By knights in shining armor.

What most fail to determine
Is the quality of the heart
That beats beneath that armor.

Scars

We are proud
Of our battle scars –
Signs of courage
And strength.

They are reminders
That we have fought
For what is right.

But there are
Other scars.

And we are ashamed
Of these hidden wounds –
Signs of cowardice
And weakness.

They are reminders
That we have surrendered
To the mistress of the night.

Rape

I witnessed a rape today.

You'd never guess
The college library
Was the scene of the crime.

I saw him
Lick his lips
When she approached.

And as she passed by
I watched –
He stripped her,
Removed her clothes,
Piece by piece.

And then –
O God!
That fire in his eyes,
That unholy burning!

But she never knew a thing
As she turned and
Went down an aisle,
Out of sight.

He smiled
And released her
From his brutal grip,
From his vile gaze,
And waited
For his next victim.

T. Jason Vanderlaan

Just One Glance

It was just
A harmless video,
A guiltless pleasure.

It was only natural,
Nothing to be ashamed of,
Right?

It was just one glance.

He is not married yet and
Things would be different then.

But now –
Now he is young
And free
And…

(Lies!)

Oh, that he could take one glance
Into his future
And see –

His wife:
Weeping and weeping
And weeping.

Oh, that he could take one glance!

He would shut his eyes forever
From breaking her heart.

Cannibals in the Cafeteria

Open,
Blatant,
Undeniable
Lust.

They stood behind me
As we waited in line
At the cafeteria.

We were hungry for lunch,
But they discussed
An appetite for
Female flesh.

They described her –
A piece of meat,
Just to be devoured.

And they were just waiting
For a chance
To sink their teeth in
And tear.

Open,
Blatant,
Undeniable
Lust.

And I was afraid
To turn around –
Afraid the burning hunger
In their eyes
Might look too much
Like my own.

Paper, Pixel

She is paper,
She is pixel,
She is power
Over me.

And when she
Comes to me

She requires nothing –
No risk, no love,
No more
Than just tonight.

Because
She is paper,
She is pixel,
She is power
To steal my eyes away.

And she requires
Nothing
Of me,

But takes
Everything.

Talge Open House

Christmas is a wonderful time
When we enjoy opening our dorm
To show off to the girls.

Of course, you know we hide
All our junk in closets –
Our last minute attempts
To show you our clean side.

But unwashed clothes
And half-eaten bags of chips
Are not all that we hide.

Wait!
Don't come in yet.

> Down come the posters
> (Open House isn't the only time
> Women can be seen in our rooms).
>
> Down come the calendars
> (You thought we kept
> Sports cars up all year?).
>
> Away go the magazines
> (Regardless of how interesting
> The articles may or may not be).
>
> Away go our dirty little secrets
> (After all, we only want you to see
> Our best and our cleanest).

There. Now all is ready.
Come in and enjoy.

Just don't open any closets.

T. Jason Vanderlaan

My Thin Veneer

Footsteps in my ear
Whisper of your approach.

Shame moistens my eyes
And I wrap my cloak around me
To hide the seeping black blood
Soaking through my shirt.

I couldn't bear for you to see
The darkness of my wounds
For then you'd know
The color of my heart.

Your knock on the door
Is a shout in my ears.

I slip the knife under my pillow
And rise to greet you, fearing
That you'll see through me –
Through this thin veneer of hypocrisy.

Because she was here tonight
And I gave her that bitter blade
To do to me as she pleased:
Slash and stab, rip and tear.

And I think she took a piece of my soul
As she walked out the back door.

But now that you're here
I'll smile and laugh with you
As if there is not a cloud in the sky,
Nor a shadow in my heart.

But I'm dying inside,
Bleeding out my sins –
Paying the price of my betrayal.

T. Jason Vanderlaan

The Door of Ta'avah

I saw the door
Open.

He hesitated,
Clutching his chest,
Attempting to contain
The crimson stain.

I heard a voice –
Soft,
But not gentle,
Silky,
But not soothing –
Calling him to enter.

He knew
To enter would be to
Deepen the wound,
But he wanted
That momentary relief,
No matter the cost.

So he staggered in,
And the darkness welcomed
His surrender.

I saw the door
Close.

Addiction

Nauseous, I stare in revulsion
At what I've become:
Skin and hollow bones.
A bloodless heart.
Decaying soul.

I am
Disgusted.

And the worst part:
I knew better.
But once again I plodded ahead,
Jumped into the familiar darkness,
And embraced the emptiness there.

I am
Ashamed.

Now I feel so cold
And all I want is release,
But I can't call out
Or they'd see me…
Here.

I am
Alone.

So in bitter resentment
I'll loathe myself,
Deeply but stoically,
For I have become
The thing I hate the most.

I am
Addicted.

T. Jason Vanderlaan

The Dark Mistress

She wanders
Defiantly
Among the houses
Of the broken brothers,
Waiting for her chance
To strike again.

And she will strike again
As long as we continue
To open the door for her.

And we do open the door,
Countless times each day –

A lingering glance at the magazine rack,
A few quick clicks and a forbidden website,
A video played in the solitude of a late night,
A daydream taken past the boundary of purity.

The latch is unlocked,
The knob is turned,
The door is opened.

And we welcome
Our Dark Mistress.

II.

What Our Hands Have Done

A Short Lesson on How to Properly Date

Come now,
Don't be naïve.

There is nothing *wrong*
With dating around.

It is simple really:
You just find a girl
(Attractive, of course,
Popular, fun, and
If possible,
Slightly witty).

Then you just
Cut, slice, and pull.

And if the heart
Isn't quite what you'd prefer
You can put it back
And try another one.

Double Deception

Despair is thus defined:
To hold a treasure
In the palm of your hand,
Only to have it slip away,
Down through your fingers like sand.

Because half truths
Are whole deceptions,
And I can't relive
That fatal day.

So kiss me one last time,
If you can bear the taste,
And I'll walk away forever
To give you the peace you deserve.

And despair is thus defined:
I held the future
In the palm of my hand,
Only to have it slip away,
Down through my fingers like sand.

Because even white lies
Are black sins,
And I can't relive
That fatal day.

So I'll kiss you one last time,
If I can stand the taste,
And walk away forever
To give you the peace you deserve.

T. Jason Vanderlaan

A Dilemma: Used or New

Look,
It's not like I'm betraying her.
She knew this was
Just for fun.

It's not my fault
She got attached
Along the way.

At least we had a good time.
And I loved her well.

Or, at least, I loved
The way she made me feel –
Like a man,
Like a conqueror.

But she knew this was
Just for fun.

And besides,
That new girl on campus
Looks lonely.

She *needs* me.
How could I leave her
To suffer alone?

Vulnerability Abused is Innocence Stolen

I knew she wasn't ready, but
I saw that she was willing.

And I loved her
Almost as much
As I loved the way
I felt when we were close.

And nearness breeds
An unquenchable desire
To be even closer.

So I made my move
And she let me,
Like a knife plunged
Into the heart of a blossoming rose.

Caught (Red-Handed)

It takes two,
But you won't even admit that,
With your finger pointed
At her heart like a gun.

But check your own chest
For a crimson stain –
Deeper and darker than hers;
You were supposed to be the man.

But bravado faded into cowardice
And I can't help but wonder:
Where is your strength now?
And how dare you point your finger!

So prepare yourself
Like a man,
And answer me now,
If you can.

The Pursuit is No Fun If the Chase is Too Short

She wanted security –
Wanted to feel needed,
Needed to feel wanted.

But all you wanted was
The rush of the pursuit.

And her only fault was
Giving in too soon.

You stole her virgin lips,
Stole her virgin heart,

And cast her aside,
Broken and used.

T. Jason Vanderlaan

Parted Lips and Polished Lies

It began with a slow, steady
Subtle slide into susceptibility.

But it ended in a crash –
Crumbling, collapsing
Into cold, calloused compromise.

And in the silence of a broken promise
I heard a woman weeping,

For the gift that was to be hers alone
Had been given to another.

A Date with a Vampire

I'm pretty sure
All her girlfriends
Told her that outfit was
Cute and fun.

But I can guarantee
Those were not the words
He was thinking
When his eyes wrapped
Around her curves.

But it worked out for the best –
She just wanted to be loved
And he just wanted fresh blood.

And when he kissed her at the door,
It was no sign of affection.

He was just taking a nibble –
Baiting her,
Until the time came
To sink his fangs fully
Into her unprepared flesh.

If I Had Known

If I had known
Each girl I kissed
Would be a bullet to your heart
I never would have pulled the trigger.

If I had known
Each girl I gave my heart to
Would be a stab to your soul
I never would have grabbed the knife.

If I had known,
I would have waited for you.

If I had known
Each time I lusted after another,
Water would fill the pit to drown your soul
I never would have opened the floodgate.

If I had known
Each time my eyes lost their purity,
A flame would be kindled to burn your heart
I never would have lit the match.

If only I had known.

To The Wives That Are Yet To Be

We'll slit your throat
With our wandering eyes,

And burn your skin
With our wayward lips.

But that is of no
Consequence
At the moment –

This is our time to shine.
This is our time to be free.
And you only live once.

So we'll choke your heart
With our deviant hands,

And drown your love
With our shallow souls.

T. Jason Vanderlaan

III.

What Our Hearts Have Betrayed

II

What Our Hearts Have Betrayed

Confessions

We are not all
Warriors of valiant strength.

We are not all
Poets with epic hearts.

We, too, are cursed
With the decay of sin.

We are all
Less than we wish to be.

We are all
Broken and afraid.

Forgive us.

T. Jason Vanderlaan

Termites

These lonely memories
Of white faces smeared red
Are eating away at the home
I have yet to build.

The roof is already caving in
And the rain of destruction
Has begun to pour down.

These bitter regrets
Of white lilies dusted black
Are gnawing away at the home
I have yet to build.

The walls are already crumbling
And the winds of strife
Have begun to blow violently.

This unchangeable past
Of white hope washed away
Is tearing away at the home
I have yet to build.

The foundation is cracking
And the mud of desolation
Is seeping up through the floor.

Grand Opening

Red ribbons flutter
Across an azure sky
As the scissors slice
Into this grand beginning.

But we never meant to start
The very sin that just won't stop.

And regret is a bitter companion
In the vacancy of our empty hearts,

But she is the baggage
Of our dearest friend,
And she is the traveling partner
Of our momentary bliss.

And we sacrificed patience for pleasure
In an attempt to soothe the hollow ache,

But satisfaction can't be stolen or staged,
And we should know because

Red ribbons fell
Across the cold concrete
As the scissors sliced
Into this grand mistake.

Not the Man

I am not the man
You think I am.

My light is darkness
And my purity is tainted.

I'm weak
When you think I'm strong.

I'm as cold as ice
When you think I'm on fire.

My faith is in doubt
And my allegiance is betrayal.

I am not the man
You think I am.

T. Jason Vanderlaan

When That Day Comes

Everything I've done
Has been like water poured
Into the well of your eyes.

So when that terrible day comes
And I have to tell you all,
I will see the price of my sin
As it flows from your eyes.

And I know my apology
Will fail to heal your wounds,
But I can only hope
You will find forgiveness for me.

Because everything I've failed to do
Has been suspended like a knife
Above your tender heart.

So when that awful day comes
And I have to tell you all,
I will see the cost of my sin
As it falls and pierces your heart.

And I know my apology
Will fail to heal your wounds,
But I can only pray
You will find forgiveness for me.

Dear Sisters

Dear sisters,
Forgive us!

We have failed you.
We have
Hesitated and
Backtracked and
Failed to fight
For your precious hearts.

Dear sisters,
Forgive us!

And pray
That we may become
More and more
Like the Warrior-Poet of the heavens.

T. Jason Vanderlaan

Apology to My Wife

As I stand here in disgrace
I can only hope
That you will forgive
My selfish heart of stone.

For I have betrayed you
Before we even met,
And sold a piece of my heart
For a moment of pleasure.

And as I kneel here in shame
I can only plead
That you will give mercy
To my undeserving heart.

For I have been unfaithful
Before we even met,
And given away a piece of my heart
For a moment of pleasure.

The Pit

We have fallen
Again and again and again
Into this pit of betrayal.

And there is only one way out:
We must pray for our souls
And reach up
Towards the strong arm
Of grace and mercy.

And God knows
We are undeserving,
But we are in desperate need.

And we ask only this:
That you pray for us
To reach up
And grasp the strong arm
Of grace and mercy.

T. Jason Vanderlaan

IV.

To Turn Blind Eyes Towards the Light

I Would Give

I would give anything
To forget the way I looked at her,

To be able to wipe away
The lust of my heart
And be cleansed anew.

But black hearts can't be washed with tears,
No matter how hard I cry,
And I can't clean this stagnant stain.

And I would give anything
To forget the way I touched her,

To be able to wipe away
The lust of my hands
And be purified again.

But falling stars can't cleanse the darkness,
No matter how hard I wish,
And I can't turn this blood to snow.

Ivy

You made your way in,
Invited by my aching emptiness,
And covered this tower with elegance.

But I weep,
Because not all that is graceful is good,
And not all that is beautiful is benevolent.

And the subtle invasion of ivy
Can make rubble out of the strong.

Because your roots infested these stones,
Cracking and separating within,
While your delicate exterior hid your motives.

But I weep,
Because not all that is charming is chaste,
And not all that is pleasant is pure.

More Than This

She is more than this
And you know it.

Despite her cold, calloused exterior
You've seen those moments
When her soul shone through,
Revealing a sweet softness.

And I know you want
What's hidden beneath,
But cracking the clam
Will only damage the pearl.

So slow down
And think before you move
Because you're more than this
And I know it.

Despite your careless exterior
I've seen those moments
When your soul shone through,
Revealing a serene strength.

And I know you want
What's hidden beneath,
But cracking the clam
Will only damage the pearl.

Slow down, my brother,
And think this through,
Because love is more than this
And you know it.

Past, Present, and Future

Presently I must apologize
To you, my future wife,
For all my past failures.

I wanted you to be
My love, first and only,
But I traded purity for pleasure
And I'm still fighting
To get it back.

So please forgive me now,
For you will be my wife
Once the past is behind us.

And I wanted to give you
A dove, pure and true,
But I traded it for a raven's wing
And I'm still struggling
To get it back.

But I pray you will not lose hope,
For as soon as this fractured heart is mended
I'll be there with you, wholly yours.

T. Jason Vanderlaan

Can't I Go Back?

Can't I go back
For just one more
Taste of tainted tonic?

I know it is poison
But I miss the flavor,

And I know it's wrong
But I crave the rush.

So can't I have
Just one more
Sip of satin sin?

No!

These unholy longings
Must be cut off.

I cannot stay here
In the land of the lifeless,
And I will not fill this emptiness
With her toxins again.

Grace

This has got to be
The most ungraceful
Start to a new beginning
You've ever seen.

With me –
The foolish one:

Stumbling,
Turning,
Forgetting,
Falling,
Crawling.

And You –
The faithful One:

Forgiving,
Encouraging,
Strengthening,
Upholding,
Carrying.

This has got to be
The most grace-full
Start to a new beginning
I've ever seen.

Return

I have greeted darkness
With a smile,
And I have wandered
In its depths –

O God,
I have wandered!

But You have never,
Never left me.
And You persistently plead
With me:

"Return!"

And I have heard
Your still, small voice
Calling.
You pursue me relentlessly.

O God,
Give me ears to hear!

And a heart to follow.

Sleeping in Gethsemane

You once told Peter –
Spirit willing, flesh weak –
To keep watch, lest he sleep.

I fall short of even his failure –
Spirit weak, flesh even weaker –
And I've been sleeping for years.

But even in my dreams
I see You coming,
Fighting for my heart.

Yet I continue on,
Secure in my slumber,
Despite promises of purity
And knowledge of the light.

I'm sleepwalking,
Stubborn and confused,
Spewing out excuses
Along this path of destruction.

Stop me, Lord!
I need You.

Wake me!

And create in me
A clean heart, O God,
And teach me to hate
The sin I love so much.

T. Jason Vanderlaan

The Slow Path of Restoration

Some tables take years to turn
And every day I fight to spurn
The stare of hollow eyes
And the venom of sweet lies.

So this is a prayer for strength
To fill my pulsing veins,
And even now I feel it returning.

And some bridges take years to burn
As every day I have to learn
The patience of slow decay
And the way of hope delayed.

But ash is as inevitable
As the fire in my heart,
And I can feel it yearning.

V.

Water For Our Hands,
Blood For Our Souls

My Last Hope

My love has grown cold
In the winter of my selfishness,
And I cannot bring spring
No matter how hard I try.

You are my last hope
To turn this life around.

So take my love and turn it to gold
In the fire of Your holiness,
Because I cannot burn away the dross,
No matter how hard I try.

You are my last hope.

T. Jason Vanderlaan

But For This Leprosy

Huddled in shadows of shame,
I hear You calling into my darkness –
Calling me toward something bold and brave.

And I could be
A valiant soldier,
But for this leprosy
Eating away at my flesh.

So wash me in the Jordan,
Cleanse me in healing waters,
And I will be whole again.

I stand and limp into the light,
Longing for something more –
Dying for more than this decay.

Because I could be
A mighty warrior,
But for this lust
Eating away at my soul.

So wash me in the Jordan,
Cleanse me in healing waters,
And I will be pure again.

Downpour From Above

Purifying rain,
Please fall down,
Wipe off this slate
And give me a new start.

Because I cannot forget
These tainted memories
Without you.

Cleansing rain
Please come down,
Wash away this scum
And give me new eyes.

Because I cannot see
Past these memories
Without you.

T. Jason Vanderlaan

Love Must Come First

I'll admit I never knew
The ocean was so vast.

And I've been trying to sail this ship
With the breath of my own lungs,
But it's only the wind of Your love
That can fill these sails again.

So come, Lord Jesus,
I need You now.

And I'll admit I never knew
This pit was so deep.

Because I've been trying to climb
With the strength of my broken bones,
But it's only the rope of Your love
That can pull me out again.

So come, Lord Jesus,
I need You now.

T. Jason Vanderlaan

The Mystery of Miracles

There is a mystery to miracles –
Paradoxes of power and patience,
And the unfathomable grandeur
Of the Lord's mercy and grace.

Because who would have thought
That fire could restore my life?
Yet He has burned me clean.

So I will raise my hands –
Proclaiming the goodness of God,
And the unexplainable majesty
Of His eternal love and truth.

And who would have thought
Blood could wash away my stains?
Yet He has covered and cleansed me.

Penance, Punishment, and the Path

I kneel here and
Plunge my hands
Into these icy waters.

And this isn't the Jordan
But these waters are cleansing my leprosy.

Because I came here for
Penance or punishment,
But found the path
To purity instead.

So I kneel and
Bring the water to my eyes
As I am purified.

And this isn't the Jordan
But these are the shores of the Promised Land.

Because I came here for
Penance or punishment,
But found the path
Away from my past instead.

Fallen

I have fallen.

To the heights
I have climbed,
But to the depths
I have –

Tumbled,
Flailed,
And screamed,
All the way to the bottom.

There, broken,
I wept.

But You have come
With a gentle hand
To restore my shattered bones.

And You have come
With a soft voice, whispering,
"My grace is sufficient."

You have helped me stand again,
But all I can do is worship –
Here at Your feet,
In all my thankfulness,

I have fallen.

Dragon Skin

I've put on this dragon skin –
Layer by layer,
Night after night.

And now You're here
With lion paws
And piercing claws
To save me from myself.

O God!
You dig so deep.

O God!
You tear so much.

But hear my prayer:
Do not stop
Until I am wholly severed
From the beast
I've grown to be.

T. Jason Vanderlaan

VI.

The Way Back Starts Not With a Step, But With a Stand

So my question is this: what are you doing *now* – mentally, emotionally, physically, spiritually – to invest in the quality of your future marriage?

Of course, the idea of preparing for marriage even before your wedding day doesn't solve all pre-marital problems. Delayed gratification can still be a difficult process. And where to draw the line between developing a current relationship and saving yourself for your future spouse can be confusing at times.

But, in my own experience, the idea of cherishing my future spouse has helped me to shift my focus away from myself. If I believe that one day I'll meet someone who I'll spend the rest of my life with, then reserving certain aspects of myself in the present no longer becomes a burdensome barrier, but rather a way for me to love my spouse – before I even meet her!

Or, if I believe the person I'm with is someone I'll want to marry (which, in my opinion, is the only good reason to date), then, as hard as it may be at times, I can have patience because I know I'll have my whole life to share with her and that I don't have to do it all right now. It can be a gradual process as the relationship grows.

And if somehow I don't end up with that person, then at least I know that I've treated her respectfully. After all, if she isn't my true love, then she is likely to be someone else's, and I want to honor her and her future spouse, just as

I hope that my future spouse is honoring me and being honored by others.

In the end, there are so many complications and variables that it can seem like too much to handle. If so much about our future marriages rests on what we are doing now, and if we make so many mistakes in the present, how can we ever hope to be happy?

It is not my goal to discourage you with all these ideas about honoring your spouse ahead of time. To be sure, we have all messed up and hurt those we love, and we will continue to do so from time to time. But with God, there is always mercy and forgiveness. And more than that, there is renewal. Though we stray from the path, if we ask God and put our trust in Him, He will always be there to guide us back to where He wants us to be.

The amount of times we've failed is not as important as the true desire of our heart to honor God and our future spouses. King David made a multitude of mistakes, and yet he was considered a man after God's own heart. I think this is because he always returned to God and allowed God to forgive and renew him.

We, too, can have that kind of relationship with God. As we learn to trust God with every aspect of our relationships, we'll find that although He doesn't always remove every obstacle or difficulty, He will always do whatever is best for us. And as His love grows in our hearts, we will be able to share that love with others, including our future spouses.

The Final Word: Grace

Whenever the topics of purity and holy living come up, there can be the tendency to feel overwhelmed. If you're anything like me, you feel like you've utterly failed in every possible way.

Sometimes I feel like I don't care about anyone but myself, and I act accordingly. Other times I feel like I have all the right ideas about how to live a holy life, but most of the time I am unable to follow through on those principles.

I don't know where you are in your life, but whether you're leading a decently good life with only a few mistakes or whether you've plunged into unspeakable darkness, we've all fallen short of the righteousness God desires for us.

If God's standards are so high, how can we ever hope to reach them? The truth is: we can't.

Now, at first that may sound like the worst news in the world, but in actuality it is the best. Once we realize that the intensity of our efforts, the nobility of our intentions, and the passion of our promises all fail to lift us to heaven, we can then fall at the foot of the cross of Jesus Christ.

There we realize that our list of good works is just as useful (or useless) as our list of sins. There we realize that all our attempts at holiness lead us to exactly the same place as when we're running from God as fast as we can. There we realize that although we are unable to produce true righteousness in our own hearts, there is a Savior who offers us His mercy and grace. He alone can redeem us and give us a chance to live a new life.

But after you accept Christ's forgiveness and as you continue in your Christian walk, I encourage you not to leave grace behind. Grace is not only the beginning of salvation, but the end and everything in between.

You'll find that there are times when you will stumble and fall. And you will fall hard. You will fall time and time again. It is part of the growing process, but it will feel like utter failure, like you'll never be able to rise again.

But in that very moment, in that very place where dirt and blood and tears mix together, that is where Jesus will wrap His arms around you and you will know that His grace is all you need.

And because grace is the only thing in the world that can raise you to your feet when you have no strength to stand, grace is also the only means to redemption. Your own good deeds can never raise you high enough; your own failed attempts can never sink you low enough. But grace can and will always raise you higher.

It is my hope and prayer that you will put your faith in Jesus, that you will put yourself in His arms of love, and let Him be your strength, now and always.

Unspoken Confessions

T. Jason Vanderlaan

Acknowledgments

I would like to give my utmost thanks to the following people for helping me edit this book: Jess Shimer, Matthew Lucio, and Mrs. Helen Pyke. Your thoughts and comments have pushed me to make this the best it can be.

I'd also like to thank two of my other fellow poets, Beth-Anne White and Kayla McAuliffe. Your writings have inspired and challenged me to be a better writer.

Thanks to everyone who has encouraged and helped me along the way – my family, my creative writing and Writer's Club friends from Southern, my poet friends, and countless others. I am where I am because of you.

Additional thanks go out to Beth-Anne White and Trudy Shiroma Koeffler for their editorial help with the extra two chapters of this second edition. Also, many thanks to all the bloggers who gave me feedback on the original version of the kissing essay.

I'm also so grateful to everyone who supported this book when it was first released, and to everyone who helped promote it. I'm especially indebted to Jay Cole for all the opportunities he gave me and for opening so many doors.

I also want to thank with all my heart those of you who have stood beside me during my own struggles, especially my fellow warriors in this great battle. The fellowship of our brotherhood has given me the strength to face each day anew. You know who you are and I just want you to know that your friendships have been the difference between life and death for me.

And last but not least, I would like to thank my Lord and Savior Jesus Christ. Without Him, this would only be half a book. He is the light in the darkness that gives me renewed hope each day. I pray that each of you will turn your eyes upon that Light and never look away.

~ ~ ~

For more information, please visit:

www.jasonvanderlaan.com

www.balmandblade.com

Pardon Me (But I'm Not Sorry)

Pardon me,
But I've come to take what's mine.

You've done your job
And kept the bargain,
Though I think our contract
Was not what you claimed.

So pardon me,
But I've come to take my heart back.

You did your job,
Cold and calloused,
But I think your promise
Was poisoned from the start.

So pardon me,
But I've come to leave.

T. Jason Vanderlaan

The Tables Have Turned

There was a time when
I would lay myself out,
Stretched on the table
For you to take your cut.

And all I asked
Was that you'd promise
To numb the pain,
At least for the night.

But now –
Now I cannot stay
Another moment.

And never again
Will I place myself
On this altar of emptiness

For your pleasure,
Or mine.

Ta'avah (We Meet Again)

And so we meet again.
It's been a while, but
I won't look you in the eyes –

They always led me down
Into the pit of your heart,
So dark and cold.

You frown at my resistance.

And I smile,
Not for you,
But because I know
I can walk away
From your icy, empty stare.

And you will be left to brood
Over your failure to devour.

I am yours no longer.

T. Jason Vanderlaan

My Midnight Kiss

The clock is ticking away the end
As a new beginning approaches.

But my New Year's kiss
Will have to wait until another time,
When I have found you
And you have found me
In holy matrimony.

But for tonight,
As I stand beneath these stars,
The only thing on my lips
Is a prayer that your heart
Will be blessed with peace and joy.

And for tonight,
As I stand under this dark sky,
My lips will only be brushed
By the soft night air,
Carrying my prayer to the heavens.

And my midnight kiss
Will have to wait until a different year,
When you have found me
And I have found you
In a love that is true.

Because the clock is ticking away our pasts
As the day when we're together approaches.

I Could Not Betray Eve Again

She stood, waiting
With parted lips
And eager hands –

An open invitation
To take and taste.

But willingness doesn't always shed light
On the proper path to follow,

Because Adam betrayed Eve
By giving in
To her enthusiasm
When he should have stood firm.

And sometimes we must say no
Even when she's begging for a yes.

And I could not betray Eve again
By giving in
To her offer of forbidden fruit
When she needed me to stand firm.

So she stood, waiting
With pursed lips
And empty hands

As I turned away.

Worth Waiting For

There is no surer way
To lose everything
Than to demand it all at once.

But I must admit
My heart is longing
To begin this dance with you.

So I'll bow my head
And say a prayer
For patience and purity,
Because I know
You are worth waiting for.

And there is no surer way
To lose a precious gift
Than to demand that it become yours.

But I must admit
My soul is longing
To begin this dance with you.

So I'll bow my head
And say a prayer
For patience and purity,
Because I know
You are worth waiting for.

T. Jason Vanderlaan

Eavesdropping on a Laundry Room Conversation at Midnight in the Dorm

O foolish Elijah!
There are more faithful than you knew.

Their knees are not stained
With the dirt of bowing to society's shallowness.
Their lips have not been poisoned
With the wisdom of wayward men.

They love purity
And seek the way of God.
They respect the vulnerable
And follow the path of honor.

O foolish Elijah!
There are more faithful than you knew.

Alone, We Must Certainly Perish

We were not meant
To walk this path
Alone.

So come beside me –
Side by side,
Back to back.
We'll find a way
Out of this hell.

And we were not made
To face the night
Alone.

So join me now –
Torches lit,
Hearts ablaze.
We'll burn the darkness
With our hope.

T. Jason Vanderlaan

The First Taste of Love

When you finally have
That first taste of love,
Full and deep,
You will weep –

Tears of regret
That you ever considered
Settling for less,

And tears of relief
That you did not.

Unspoken Confessions

T. Jason Vanderlaan

Afterword: My First Kiss

A light breeze glided around us, whispering a mystery. She leaned in closer. Her hair danced gently across my face, caressing my cheeks. I leaned in closer. I could taste the breath from her parted lips – a silent request for more. Our eyes closed, and then... the kiss!

Or, at least, that's how I imagine it might be like. The truth is I've never kissed a girl. But before you pity me, let me be clear: I've chosen to save my first kiss until marriage.

Now, I'm very curious to know what is going through your mind right now. Perhaps some of you still pity me. Maybe some of you admire me (though God knows I definitely don't deserve it). Some may think it is a nice but antique idea. Others may be offended, thinking I'm some kind of prude who wants to not only deprive myself of certain relational enjoyments, but also deprive everyone else as well.

But to be honest, I desire none of those responses. All I want is for you to give me a few moments and let me tell you why I've made such a choice. This will only be a basic summary, not a detailed analysis, but when we're finished I hope to have given you something to think about, whether we agree or disagree.

I. Why Should Marriage Matter to the Unmarried?

All of this begins with my concept of marriage. I believe that marriage is the most unique of all human relationships. Each type of relationship is special in its own way, but a husband and wife share more unique, private experiences, both emotional and physical, than anyone else.

For simplicity sake, we're just going to look at the physical aspects of relationships, and even then, more narrowly focused on the American culture in which I live. I realize these things may vary from culture to culture a bit.

There are certain acts that are common to human interactions – hugs, touching hands (handshakes, an act of comfort, holding hands in prayer or song, etc.), and so on. But there are other acts which are exclusive to husband and wife – primarily but not limited to sex of any kind. These interactions not only emphasize and enhance the intimacy of the marriage relationship, but also its uniqueness. By choosing to refrain from these exclusive acts outside of marriage, a person upholds the value and holiness (set-apartness) of marriage.

This commitment to uniqueness, however, begins even before marriage. For example, if you believe that sexual intercourse is exclusive to marriage, would you go around having sex with anyone you want up until your wedding day and then after that only with your spouse? Of course not! You understand that sexual intercourse is to be a unique, shared experience with your spouse *only*.

Therefore, even before marriage, you are faithful to your spouse by not having sex with anyone who isn't your spouse. This also excludes anyone you're dating or even engaged to. Unless he/she *is* your spouse, you do not have spousal rights.

Support for such a view of marriage is not very common or popular. Even among Christians who vow to abstain from sex until marriage, the idea of honoring your spouse before marriage tends to be very limited and compartmentalized.

For example, a couple may promise to wait until marriage to have sexual intercourse, but they might consider anything up to that point to be permissible. But is that really respecting the holiness of marriage? Is it only sexual intercourse that is unique to marriage or is it anything and everything sexual?

II. To Kiss or Not to Kiss?

So what does any of this have to do with kissing? Where do you draw the line between what is to be saved for marriage and what is acceptable before marriage?

The first thing I'd like to say is that the most important question isn't, "How far can I go without it being wrong?" but "How far can I go to protect the uniqueness and sacredness of marriage?" The focus should be on guarding and cherishing the heart of your future spouse.

Secondly, I'd like to suggest the following principle: Any act that is unique to the marriage relationship should be abstained from until marriage.

Basically, ask yourself this: will I be doing such-and-such with anyone but my spouse once I'm married? If the answer is no, then it is an act unique to marriage and should be saved for your spouse only… and unless you have a spouse, that means you don't get to do it yet. Or, better phrased, you get to keep that part of yourself especially for the person you marry.

Now, I'm aware that there are some grey areas and I am not advocating drawing a line between marriage and non-marriage that says "no physical contact before, even in dating." I believe that marriage is significantly different than anything before it, but I also see how dating can be a transitional phase between "just friends" and "just married." Thus, it lends itself to those types of physical interactions which gradually increase in intimacy as two people grow closer to each other.

To be clear, I'm not trying to give you step-by-step instructions on how to live your love life. Rather, I'm trying to suggest some general principles that you could apply to your own experiences. It is the responsibility of each couple to determine their boundaries within the context of purity.

None of this is to say that physical touch is bad. On the contrary, it is healthy and necessary in any intimate human relationship. It is even likely that a relationship in our culture might suffer from a complete denial of physical expression. But that doesn't negate the truth that some interactions are to be reserved only for the marriage relationship.

Let's look at a couple examples of how this might look in real life.

Exhibit A: Hugging. Once you are married, you will continue to hug people other than your spouse. Therefore, a basic hug is not unique to marriage, and can be shared with your significant other before marriage.

Of course, as a couple grows closer, the intimacy of hugs may increase. Since it is so difficult to determine when a hug becomes too intimate for dating, it is the responsibility of the couple to draw a line that protects the uniqueness of marriage.

Exhibit B: Kissing. Once you are married, you will not kiss anyone on the lips except your spouse. Therefore, it is an act unique to marriage, and should be saved for your spouse alone. In some cultures, a person might kiss someone they're not married to – for example, their child – but this is clearly different than the romantic kiss we're referring to here. Since it is easy to see the intended intimacy of such a kiss, it should be saved until marriage.

In other words, you could argue forever about the fuzzy line between a "regular hug" and a "romantic hug," and so I believe these grey areas of physical intimacy must be determined on a personal basis through communication between the couple during the transitional phase of dating.

However, no such argument can take place about kissing on the lips. Such a kiss, as shared by a couple, is always romantic; it is therefore not a grey issue and does not belong in the transitional phase of dating. Instead, it and other such interactions are to be saved for the uniqueness of marriage.

III. What Really Matters Here?

Obviously, these are very simple examples, and real life is much more complicated. But I hope you get the idea of protecting the uniqueness of marriage even before you're married. Until the day you marry your girlfriend, she is not your wife. Until the day you marry your boyfriend, he is not your husband.

Mainly we've focused on the physical side of relationships, but this also applies to emotional intimacy. In fact, I think that the physical and emotional sides of our being are so interwoven that sometimes we do a disservice by discussing them as if they are wholly separate. So whether we're talking about our bodies or our emotions, what we're really talking about is how our thoughts and actions affect not only our own hearts, but each other's hearts as well.

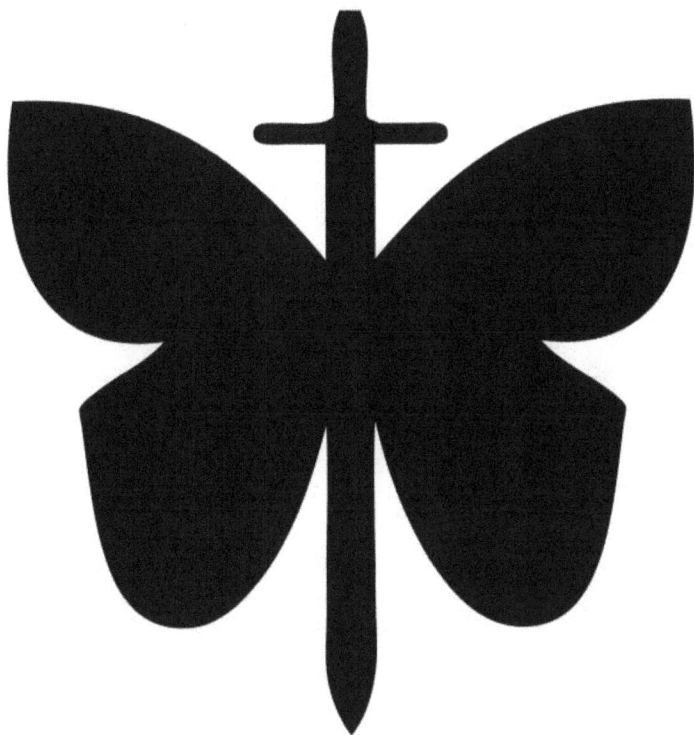

For the latest news and updates
from Balm and Blade Publishing,

please visit our blog:
balmandblade.blogspot.com

or join us on either
Facebook or MySpace.

www.ingramcontent.com/pod-product-compliance
Lightning Source LLC
Chambersburg PA
CBHW051043030426
42339CB00006B/180